"I will be Mum," said Helen.

"And I will be in the shoe shop," said Adam.

"Do you have shoes for me?"
said Helen.

"Do you like the party shoes?" said Adam.

"No," said Helen.

"Do you like the red shoes?" said Adam.

"No," said Helen.

"Do you like the big shoes?"
said Adam.

"No," said Helen.

"Do you like the small shoes?" said Adam.

"Yes," said Helen.

"They are your shoes, Helen," said Adam.